Country Charm
COLORING BOOK

TERESA GOODRIDGE

DOVER PUBLICATIONS, INC.
MINEOLA, NEW YORK

Welcome to country living at its best! The horses and cows and cats and dogs are lazing in the pasture and under the old oak tree. The laundry is hanging on the line in the cool summer breeze, and family and friends are enjoying the outdoors with ice cream and refreshing glasses of lemonade from the country store. Add your colors to the thirty-one picturesque scenes by artist Teresa Goodridge. Plus, the perforated pages make it easy for you to showcase your works of art!

Bibliographical Note

Country Charm Coloring Book is a new work, first published
by Dover Publications, Inc., in 2018.

International Standard Book Number

ISBN-13: 978-0-486-82168-9
ISBN-10: 0-486-82168-4

Manufactured in the United States by LSC Communications
82168406   2019
www.doverpublications.com

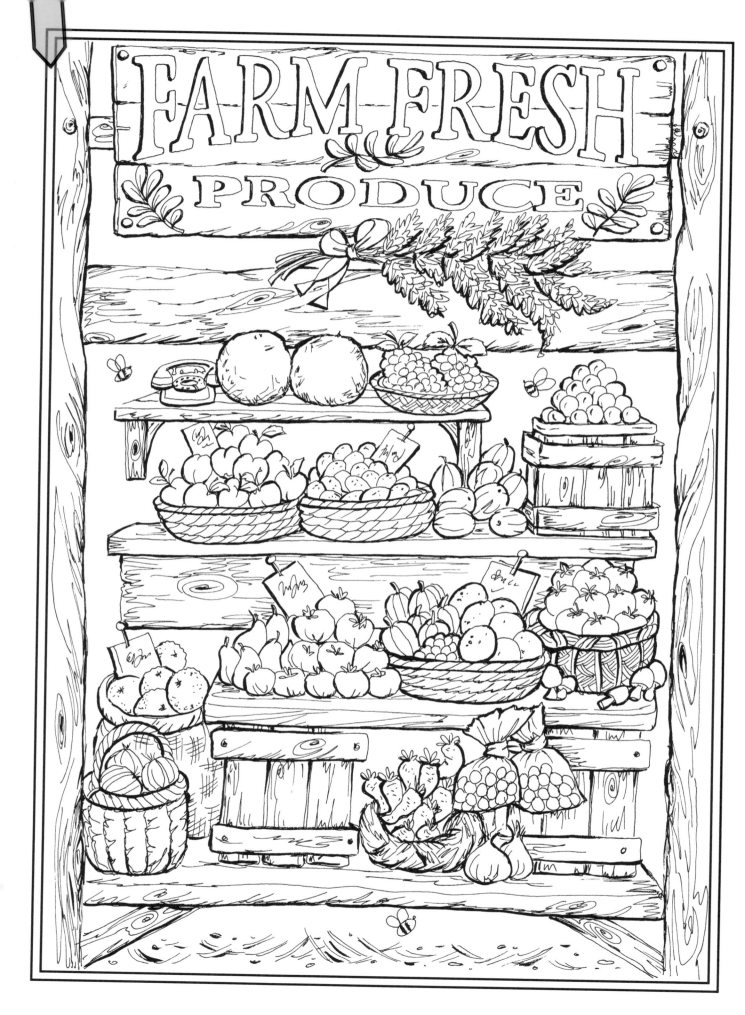

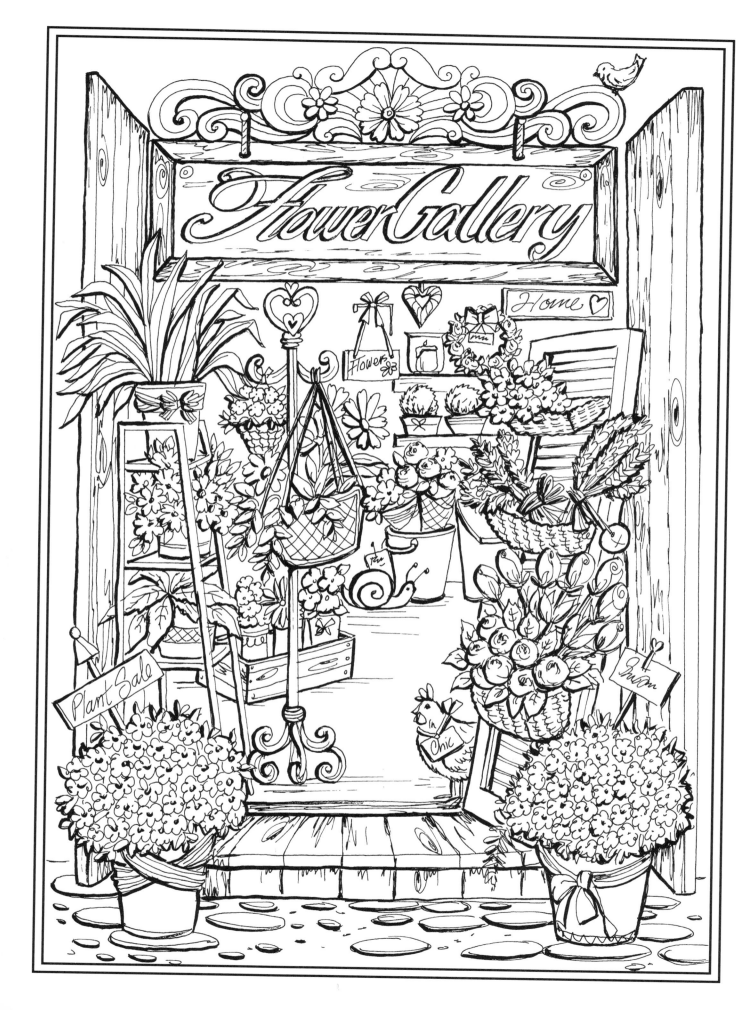